A Lesson in Forgiveness

By

Stacy

Believing

Giving Your All

There comes a time when you must face the truth, face your fears, and live your remaining years facing toward them and not away from them if you want to get to where you envision your life. It isn't easy for many, but that doesn't make it impossible. In fact, the only way to make through it is knowing you cannot run from it. It is when your only choice is to face the truth that you can move toward it head on.

There's always a lesson to learn on such journeys. I went through a lot, but I never let anything get in my way. I listened to myself, only and entirely, and fought tooth and nail to not let the tragedies defeat or overpower me.

I have learned that belief in yourself and everything you say is the key to winning in life. People will try to put you down to keep you stuck in the most despicable ways. But believing in your future as you want it, and not as what is dealt to you, will get you through every hurdle. How else can you expect to win in life if you don't believe success to be your goal, your load, and the power you hold?

Believe in yourself and give your all in everything you do, because your belief in yourself makes you stronger than you can ever imagine.

My Stability

My heart has many things to say to you. Though they cannot be summed up in a simple phrase, I will give them to you in several small ways.

You are My King, my fuel, my light, my kiss in the morning and night.

I love you…deeply and thank you for understanding my hard life.

Your smile radiates my day. You give me butterflies, and to this day, you still make my heart jump.

Thank you for always taking care of me. Even as we both strengthened each other each day, you pushed me to pursue my goals on days I didn't think I had it in me.

So, thank you, my love, my friend, and my credit. Without you, this wouldn't be placed in motion. Here I go…all in or nothing, as we say!

Table of Contents

Chapter 1 - Beginning

Growing up in a fun household is every child's dream, and so it was Stacy's. Her dreams were fulfilled by her mother, who, despite being a schizophrenic, made her life interesting. But on the other hand, her father, who was mentally, physically, and emotionally incapable of showing compassion, made her life a living hell.

A military attitude is important to have, even if one is not in the military. It keeps you disciplined and shows people that you are respectful, honorable, and efficient. However, too much of anything can be harmful, especially for children.

Parents can make or break their children's personality. They can even alter it. Stacy's experiences from her childhood would permanently alter how she governs herself when she becomes a woman, as well as how she bonds with others.

Stacy has an attitude of not letting anyone get close to her. She makes it impossible for anyone to find out anything about her or her family. Often, she tells herself she is shutting off from nonsense, yet she wonders what about her makes those close to her bring so much drama into her life.

Let's backtrack a bit and see how Stacy's life got affected.

It all started somewhere that will never escape her mind: the noise around the base where she was raised. It was the kind of place where everyone knew everyone. In fact, it was the kind of place where everyone knew everything about everyone. But, despite that, nobody came to anyone's rescue. They didn't allow those in need of help to receive any help from the outside, either.

Like in many homes on the base, abuse was common in Stacy's home. Her father was insultingly abusive to her mom and to the family in many ways. Why? Stacy could never learn the answer to that question. During her early years, she assumed it to be her mother's illness or the drugs keeping a cloud on her father's heart and mind.

Her father would often come home and not speak to anyone. He would enter the home and head straight toward his room. Her mom was always on tiptoes at the time of his arrival. On days he would go straight to his room, Stacy's mom followed her father, almost running behind him. Stacy and her siblings were already instructed to be quiet so as not to upset their father.

It didn't matter as he would already be upset, but her mother did what she could to protect her kids. Running after her husband into the room had the same purpose. The children would hear nothing for an hour, followed by their mother's subdued whimpering.

Like her siblings, Stacy didn't know what happened at the time. But as she grew up, she realized her mother was trying to calm her father. Her mother made sure to keep the children safe and happy. But it wasn't always easy.

It was overwhelming for Stacy, too. She knew it would always be that way and a challenge. While Stacy's mother succeeded in protecting Stacy, at least for a while, Stacy didn't know how difficult it was for her mother.

As Stacy grew up, the frequency with which her father returned home in a pissed mood increased. Over time, it got out of control for her mother, too. Her behavior had become unsteady and erratic both due to her mental illness and the abuse she had to tolerate from her husband's hands for years.

It got to the point that Stacy's mother would tell the children to go outside before their father's return in the evenings, ask the kids to go outside and play instead of telling them to watch television or go to their rooms. *Out of sight, out of mind,* she thought.

Being a tomboy and fond of rough sports, Stacy didn't mind going outside anytime. However, going outside also came with unwanted consequences. See, Stacy's father didn't like dirty children. For him, stepping outside the house meant getting dirty, and he was the type of person who, if he thought his children were dirty, subjected them to consequences. This meant a bath by him with Clorox in the water, a tormenting and ruthless bathing ritual he got off on.

Chapter 2 - You'll Always Be Wrong

She had to deal with her father's quirks from the age of five, so Stacy had come to expect the worst. If she got the opportunity to go outside, Stacy took it despite her father's issue with dirt. It did make her wonder if he had to grow up with some form of bathing torture as well. Anyway, Stacy went outside and enjoyed her time with her friends. She just knew how to expect the unexpected because of a life lesson she had learned.

Stacy knew what he would want her to do when he came home. She would prepare herself for a bath from her father, who believed an average bath to include harsh chemicals.

"Take off your clothes and get in the tub, Nikki," Stacy's father would order. After making sure he cleaned her pussy thoroughly, he would hand Stacy a soapy wash rag and order her to get clean again, inside and out. He made her do this every night. "Plus," he would add, "This would help tone down your dark complexion."

Nikki was not her name; her name was Stacy. But her father called her Nikki to feel more in control over her. He knew he could call his daughter with a name that didn't belong to her, yet she would comply. Stacy believed it was a turn-on for him to be in control. Hearing this name from others felt degrading. The worst part about it was that he called Stacy 'Nikki' behind closed doors. Nikki became an intricate, and permanent, part in Stacy's life; Nikki and Stacy became cemented together like Siamese Twins.

That was it in a nutshell. The root of the issue was Stacy's skin tone. "Black and dark as Hell itself," as her father would belt out disgustedly. That was how he described his own daughter, and the remedy was to bathe her with water containing Clorox. It didn't matter if it burned her eyes, nose, private areas, or her skin. That was what he wanted, and nothing else mattered to him.

Stacy wished she was born a shade lighter. She hated that her black skin tone was the cause of evil done to her. *Lighter skin would solve everything,* she often thought. If only she was a tad lighter, maybe her father wouldn't touch her. But then, if he was so repulsed by her skin, why did he touch her at all? It didn't make any sense.

Stacy's father was a solid two hundred and fifty pounds, six foot one, African American man who was just as dark yet hated the color black. He cussed at his family often, in a drunk or drug-induced rage, expressing his hatred for whatever made him mad that day.

If Stacy wore bright colors, he would quickly pass a painful remark. "You know you are not light enough to wear that color, Nikki. Come on now, I shouldn't have to remind you," he would say, laughing. "Look in the mirror, dammit!"

Shouting was normal in her home. It appeared to Stacy it was the only way her father knew how to get his point across. Of course, most shouting occurred about cleaning, cooking, not following his orders, not answering a question he asked, and skin color they dared to continue to have. It was a deep-rooted subject for Stacy's father. Her baths took about thirty to forty minutes by her father. Stacy pondered if her father had the same bath routine as he imposed on her. Still, to this day, she wonders if growing up that's how he was made to bathe.

At the age of eight, Stacy was put on display, as if her father wasn't shy to show the world that he was embarrassed by his black daughter.

Stacy had come home crying. Although she knew coming home crying was an ingredient for trouble, she had assumed she would be safe this once as it was too early in the day for her father to be home. She had done nothing wrong and only wanted to feel protected behind a locked door. But she couldn't get what she needed, as that day, unfortunately, her father was home.

Crying was a weakness, and being weak, especially showing it, wasn't allowed in her household.

Coming home from school, Stacey jumped off the school bus. James, an asshole of a boy who lived on base with his parents as well, enjoyed calling her names as she walked past him. "Hey! Tar baby. Blackout." Stacy couldn't escape the insults from inside her own home nor outside the home. "Smile, Stacy, show your teeth. Light our way through the dark." Kids can be so cruel.

Stacy learned that emotional, mental, and psychological torment can take a physical toll on the spirit, soul, and health of a person. Her father was not the only one casting a negative impact in her life, any and every one became a bully in Stacy's life. Words hurt; they cut deeply; and Stacy found herself around those characters throughout her early life.

James decided to go beyond being mean that day. He became violent. He stabbed Stacy in the head with a lead pencil. Stacy ran. She found her father sitting on the couch as she entered the house crying. He saw his daughter crying and said, "What the hell?" Between snot and tears, Stacy tried to explain, hoping her father would help or protect her.

Nope! He slung open the door and said, "Get your black ass back out there now!" Stacy wasn't expecting this, nor were other kids, including James, who had followed Stacy to her home and stood in her yard. Their mouths

8

dropped open. "Oh Hell," muttered James. He knew Stacy's father had a temper. His dad and Stacy's dad were drinking buddies and indulged in other things together, too.

Stacy's father called him out, "Oh, you like hitting girls, huh? Okay, kick her ass now." All Stacy could think was, *who is he to speak about placing his hands on anyone? Hypocrite.* She and James scrapped outside in the yard as her father and the other kids watched. She held her own that day. It was a good one. She had stood up for herself. She hoped her father was proud of her.

That night, Stacy heard footsteps coming toward her room. She kept her eyes shut. Slowly, the door opened. Stacy's father came inside and unzipped his jeans. They dropped to the floor. He then grabbed Stacy and put her in the sitting position. He placed Stacy's hands between his legs. She didn't say anything. She was asleep, after all. He didn't care, and Stacy didn't want to completely wake up because he wasn't going to go away. She wished and pretended it to be a nightmare.

Stacy's father usually bothered her only on the weekends, not school days. But as of late, he had been doing drop-in two nights every week plus weekends.

She opened her mouth and started sucking her father's dick. She didn't resist, though she wanted to. Her wish was to not upset her father. First and foremost and above and beyond everything else, she never wanted to do anything wrong.

"You are getting good at making that monster come, Nikki," he gloated.

She jumped up without being told and went to clean herself up.

Upon coming back to her room, she found her father still there. Why? She looked at him with questioning eyes, wondering what he wanted with her now.

Smack! "Don't ever walk away from me until you are told."

Stacy was dumbfounded. It was unbelievable that she was somehow always wrong. Obedient or defiant, she was still incorrect.

Stacy went to her shoe box of a cubby hole that she went to when things became hard to handle and she needed to release her anger. Stacy had a nice size closet; and way back in the corner of her closet was an area where she could hide and if someone looked in there, no one could see her. So, she called it her "Cut and Hide Room."

Stacy sat in this cubby and wrote in her journal, something she'd been doing since she was seven or eight. Once she was done, she topped it off by rolling a dice she had stolen from one of her sister's game Shoot. She only needed one, not two. She would roll the dice and the number it landed on was the number of times she would cut. The higher the number, the harder it is to hide the cuts. Stacy was a self-mutilator. She didn't have anyone to turn to about the situation. It was mind-boggling to her that her family knew her father was abusive toward her mother, yet they never thought to sit Stacy down and check on the kids. Nope! So, Stacy cut to ease the pain away. Cutting was a tool for Stacy, like shouting, to express herself.

Some of the most significant components of a person's individuality include self-esteem, confidence, and mental strength. These components are also essential to preserving their fundamental beliefs and values.

The way Stacy was raised, she had no clue what she was born to strive for in life. She was left confused and defeated by the one person who was supposed to nurture and protect her. In place of love and support, the closed-mindedness and inconsistent emotions she felt were what developed her sense of self.

Stacy began to shut down. It happened to her in more ways than expected. She suppressed her feelings by actively participating in everything she could. Decades later, she would ask herself, "Was it real?"

There were several opportunities for her to pursue improvement. But she didn't have a clue as to how or where to start. Simply put, it didn't take long for her to achieve maturity, added by her father's hands, as he would hit her and call her ugly.

Children don't think badly of anything until they are told something is bad. Her own father telling her she is ugly, along with calling her disgusting words, robbed Stacy of her self-esteem and innocence. It made her the person she is today.

Though she appears an extrovert, as she easily becomes the center of attention wherever she goes, she doesn't like to draw attention to herself. People get drawn to her for her charisma and humor. But she likes nothing more than being in her own company. There weren't many people in her life she could call her friends, though she was friendly with everyone she came across in her life.

She believes it could be her coping mechanism to always be cheerful around people so nobody could have a reason to question her intentions. Why expose her true views or motives to the world? No one will really understand how she truly feels inside anyway. So, keeping certain thoughts to herself felt much safer. Exposing herself will only show nothing but weakness. This made Stacy strong-minded and kept her believing within herself that if no one had her back, she would never be hurt ever again.

Reminiscing now, Stacy can see she was a strong-minded child. That occurrence was one of many events that taught her to never back down or surrender. Let's just say, it wasn't the last time she was tested. She remembered even the things that hurt.

Her father knew that she detested mice, but he would lock her in the kitchen closet, with mice inside, for hours on hours as punishment. When he thought she was being defiant, he would tuck her into bed with mice in the sheets. He enjoyed tossing mice at her for amusement. This was just to watch her cry. She knew her father was a narcissist; he got his rocks off on controlling his family.

Stacy's father not only defiled her sexually, at times he also made her cause bodily harm on her mother; he would make Stacy whip her mother with a belt. When Stacy couldn't do it, Stacy's mother would beg her to just do it, because if she didn't, her husband, i.e., Stacy's father, would turn it around on Stacy and beat her instead.

Stacy's father was a sadistic pertinent that when the family sat down to watch a movie, he would make her rub his member under the covers. He did it all and several other things that made her feel like shit. He made her try cocaine and marijuana and made her drink so she would 'loosen up.' Humiliation was his favorite form of torture.

Yet, Stacy was always headstrong. Despite it all, she engaged in conflicts with her father which made her life even more difficult, as he constantly tested Stacy.

Stacy has known suffering, and struggle and loss from a young age, yet she found her way out of the depths of hell to beauty. Above all, she learned that in order to heal, one must forgive. Stacy knew that her childhood wasn't normal and that she was different from most other children her age. But she thinks that the important thing was that she started to discover that she still had a lot more in common with many others.

Stacy scrimmaged with her father on several occasions growing up. She did so to rebel against all sorts or torture he inflicted on her; with sexual encounters, color, attitude, drugs, and other forms of abuse, or just her father attacking her character to lower her self-esteem.

She always told herself she had the choice to become whoever and whatever she wanted and wasn't defined by what was happening to her or had happened to her.

Stacy loved the movie Gladiator, for it showed how one can and must stand against wrong and evil for their right. She watched it many times growing up, gaining the motivation to keep going every time she did.

She also read various books, especially on philosophy, to understand her situation better and make the best of the resources she had. She especially liked reading Marcus Aurelius. His words, "You have power over your mind, not outside events. Realize this, and you will find strength," became the source of stability at many points in her life.

She understood early in life that all she could do was learn from her mistakes and hope that she wouldn't regret her actions as much as she regretted her then-present. Stacy knew she couldn't change what was already done, go back in time, or undo the hurt caused to her.

She motivated herself with quotes to empower her self-conscious everyday her father demonized her spirit. She reminded herself that she was not alone, and that no matter what she went through, she could cope with it. Stacy couldn't trust friends, family members, counselors, or therapists about her situation, but she could trust herself and those who had come before her and succeeded against the struggles of life. It was as If cut out the middleman syndrome. Trust who you know, and it just so happens to be her only without no hesitation.

Stacy knew she deserved to be happy and healthy, and that she had the potential to achieve her goals and dreams. Her father wasn't the only obstacle in her way. In fact, an even bigger hurdle would be her self-doubt. Thus, as much as she doubted herself whenever she allowed him to evade her memories, she had to remain strong.

He belittled her, called her names, and put her down. He enjoyed humiliating and embarrassing her in front of people. He mentioned regularly how he was in control, threatening to harm her body. He used to force his personal sexual fantasies on her while monitoring her reaction to his horror. Yet, Stacy identified and challenged her negative thoughts.

Sometimes, a negative view or perception is based on irrational or distorted beliefs and can make things worse. Though Stacy knew her negative perception was valid, she kept her optimism. She knew negative perceptions can be unavoidable at times, but that trying to suppress or ignore them makes them stronger.

Stacy tried, as best as she could, to identify and challenge her negative impressions, and replace them with more balanced and optimistic ones. She knew pessimistic lines of thinking can be unpleasant and distressing, so she could not let them be permanent or takeover her emotions. She tried different strategies to forget and cope with her negative thoughts, depending on the nature and intensity of her shame, to maintain her strength, stability, and sanity.

Yet, her father often made it difficult for her.

Stacy created her own destiny.

In many lonely moments, even to this day, she wonders if she ever crossed his mind. Was she a fool to still wish for a normal life, hoping for someone to stand by her through thick and thin and offer unconditional love? She hoped with anticipation, by thinking with an open heart and not with a closed one, that the choices he made would somehow benefit her.

She ponders over how he used to say that he was showing her what real love can be. But as she reminisces, she cannot recall it feeling like love at all. She put her all in something to get no compassion in return.

She wonders when she will get what she deserves, deserved all this time. Everything she had been given gets on her nerves. Her mind is a mess full of distress, from the confusion, exhaustion, ignorance, and sickness that she received for a lack of judgment.

Yet, she created her own destiny in every way possible. She did not allow him to steal her joy or take away her spirit. She won as happiness always triumphs over evil.

Chapter 3 - Happy Birthday

Everyone's reality has many perspectives, after all. Nikki's childhood played a major part in her perception of what a normal life is.

Her childhood reality played a major part in her perception of having a normal life. Follow her as she turns her downs to ups and her frowns to smiles.

It can be done, damn it! How so, it has its point in time when it may be challenging. It can also be like soul searching for those looking for answers. Everyone has a story. This is Stacy. The good, the bad, and downright fucking unbelievable.

Regardless of what many say, being an introvert can be a lonely life. Being an introvert with extroverted moments can be even more dangerous.

Nikki remembers lying there, staring up at the ceiling. It was pitch black in her room. The day itself was amazing. Her grandfather had brought her a rocking horse for her sixth birthday. There was cake, candy, and lots of food she liked to eat. She loved it. She wondered why this beautiful day had to end this way. How did her father always find a way to fuck everything, especially good memories, beyond all recognition?

That was the one thing that was constant throughout her story: something would happen that would fuck up a good moment. This isn't, by any means, a down on her luck, but just sad for her tale. It's just what happened to her and how she turned her shit pile into a horizon. Yes! One of those with a twist.

The sounds were just too disgusting to hear; licking and groaning echoed in her closed room. It was loud to her. Why couldn't her mother hear it? Nikki knew her mother was in a deep coma-like sleep. Her father drugged or over-medicated her one or the other way.

Their house was constructed like a ranch-style home, but it was a trailer. The master bedroom was at one end, with a full bathroom, kitchen, and living room in between, and a second bedroom at the other end. So no, her mother wouldn't be able to hear a thing. Great!

Nikki was stuck there. It felt to her he was spitting on her. There were many words to describe that area. Vagina, pussy, bush, he had several words for his favorite spot.

She tried to put her hand in the way when it got too rough, though she knew better. Smack! Every time she did something that got in the way of what was being done.

He came up and said, "Touch me."

Smack! "You know not to touch it with your teeth dammit! Now wet big boy with your mouth," he whispered. "Suck tighter, shit. I shouldn't have to tell you this, Nikki. You're old enough that you know exactly how I like it. So do that damn thang!"

Okay, okay, she thought. She just had to block out her thoughts and get him out of her room. It seemed since her sister slept in the bed with her mother often, she couldn't escape him and his big boy.

He groaned and moaned in her mouth. Both his hands grabbed onto the back of her head. She wet her mouth more, squeezing and gripping his junk tight. She knew he was about to come. She just wanted him to be done with her. She pulled slightly at his balls with one hand and manipulated his shaft with her tongue.

Fucking her tiny mouth with his dick while groping and pulling at her nipples. He enjoyed every movement. She tasted him in her mouth. *Just a few more strokes and this would be over,* she thought. She sucked and pulled more. He got louder. But it didn't matter since no one was coming to stop this disaster. Nikki continued until he thrust his dick deeper into her throat. She gagged. She knew not to push away, or he would smack her.

It didn't take long until Nikki squeezed every drop out of him. Suddenly, he pulled out, spilling all over her face and chest.

"Fuck!" He spoke. "Yes. Just what I needed."

She thought he was peeing on her. It was hot and sticky. She couldn't believe it.

"Happy birthday! You're growing up, Nikki." He spoke. "Now go clean yourself up and be quiet about it."

"Okay, Daddy," was all she could say.

"Now go get cleaned up," he said.

Nikki jumped up from her bed, got cleaned, brushed her teeth, and went to bed. She had to get some sleep for school. She had become great at compartmentalizing already. It seemed to her that her mom had realized something was going on because she had begun putting them to bed earlier than usual.

It wasn't too often she slept alone in her room, but as of late, she did. Nikki didn't care. She was ecstatic about the change. But then everything started to change completely with her mother. Nikki started to wonder why my siblings didn't sleep in the same room with her anymore.

Stacy's father had more access to her without question, that's why! She felt like a complete fool. Too good to be true, damn it!

It's strange how a few short seconds can lead one's life in a whole new direction. It alters how one thinks and acts and sees their own reflection.

In a single moment, Stacy's life changed forever. Everything she had previously known had been suddenly rearranged.

Stacy remembers when she was six, her mother told her that it would be easy for the family to just let her father do what he needed to do to keep the peace in the house, until she could figure out a way to straighten things out. This is when everything started to change completely with her mother.

Stacy wonders, did her mother give her to her father like a piece of meat placed on the chopping block? Wasn't she supposed to protect her?

No one will ever understand just how I felt those days,

But through my words I hope to convey.

I cannot begin to illustrate the repulsive person I knew,

I only intend to express the horror that I went through.

He pinned me hard and rough against the concrete bed,

I didn't know what to do with what I felt.

Yet, you continued to do what you did,

You didn't just take my innocence but began to haunt my soul.

I was captured; there was no way to escape,

I wondered if I deserved it if it really was my fate.

My thoughts carried confusion; his mind was filled with lust.

He took parts of me with each thrust.

Tears ran down my face in the dark,

With a feeling of disgrace burning in my heart.

His cold touch, like a vacuum, sucked out the life in me.

His ears wide open, he ignored all my pleas.

Standing there in the night, so scared, so exposed,

Yet covered by darkness, it seeps into my head.

I felt guilty of what was being done.

It seemed so close, but it was really oh so far.

Worse than at the doctor, he injected me with filth and dirt.

His intention was deliberate, it was clear and overt.

It's a bit funny that a piece of scum is all he will ever be,

With his only accomplishment in life, doing me.

On some nights still, I cannot fall asleep.

Mourning over my innocence, that wasn't mine to keep.

What some can imagine as only their worst nightmare,

It is my reality that cannot be undone nor repaired.

I may have the sweetest smile, glowing between my nose and chin,

Only I know the truth of my sadness held within.

My pretty eyes have seen more than they should,

And cried more tears than anyone ever could.

I gained a kind heart, but it came with a cost,

It has felt the worst of pains and experienced the greatest loss.

I cannot change the past, the event to which I succumbed,

But I can focus on the present and change what is to come.

We are all different, yet same

Every one of us experiences some kind of shame.

Scattered throughout our lives, like a friend, one of a kind,

Dreary days will always follow, bad memories trailing behind.

Those dark days are necessary, just as important as the rest,

For if we didn't have the worst, we couldn't recognize the best.

I push and pull my way through life, but wat happened to me has made me a beast.

Strong in mind, strong in goals, strong in accomplishing everything I hold.

So don't let your fears be your downfall, instead, let them pull you up,

For you never know who you may inspire with life's unknown desire.

Chapter 4 - Lisa

How much does one eat? Stacy never knew how much she ate. She didn't think she ate a lot, though. But she was made to feel like she ate a lot.

She hated everything. It was unbelievable to her how her life could be this bad. Worst things, the worst of the worst, kept happening to her.

She sat motionless, recalling a statement she had heard, "Arrogance and pride can go hand in hand." Sitting motionless was the only reaction she was capable of in that moment. Looking down, she continued to read the same passage she had already read uncountable times, hoping for it to become clearer, but it didn't.

Stacy's friend Lisa came over on Fridays, as her mother worked late at the beginning of each weekend. The girls would do their weekend homework, play, bathe, eat, and go to bed. Sometimes, Lisa's mother would pick her up in the middle of the night.

Stacy enjoyed spending time with Lisa. They got along well. She wanted to tell Lisa about what her father did to her, but it felt wrong to talk about it. Stacy knew she had done nothing wrong. Regardless, it was her dad, and she didn't feel right discussing it.

One of Stacy's uncles was visiting them. It was when her mother was still around. Her uncle was difficult to understand so Stacy's mother had left him to entertain himself while she took her younger daughter to run errands.

Stacy and Lisa were the only two homes.

"Touch it," she told Lisa.

Lisa didn't move.

"Are you scared?" Stacy asked.

"Yes. Are you?"

"Nah! Why would you ask me that?"

Stacy could tell Lisa was enjoying it. Her little nipples were hard as rocks. "Just be still, I'm going to do something," said Stacy before lifting her friend's gown and licking her breasts. She wanted to see Lisa's reaction to what was done to her on the regular. She rubbed her little breasts and Lisa giggled.

Stacy stopped.

"No, Nikki. Don't stop." Lisa said.

Lisa liked it. *Weird*, thought Stacy. She hated it being done to her. She went down to Lisa's stomach with small kisses.

She was heading between her legs when the door swung open, "You girls need to…"

The girls stopped. They looked at Stacy's uncle, who had stopped mid-sentence and whose mouth was hung wide open.

"What the fuck are you doing to her, little black girl? Get the hell off her NOW!" He said as he snatched Lisa up and rushed her into the living room.

Stacy began crying hysterically. Her uncle came back but without Lisa.

"If I ever see you do something like this ever again, I will tell your dad. Do you hear me?" He screamed at Stacy.

"Yes, sir," replied Lisa between sniffles.

Stacy cried herself to sleep that night. She kept wondering why her uncle was so pissed. What had she done so wrong? Lisa wasn't upset by what she had done; she had liked it. Stacy wanted to know why Lisa had liked it when she hated it. She was so confused.

Her friendship with Lisa was crucial to Stacy. She didn't want to hurt her one bit. She had to talk to her, apologize to her if she had hurt her unknowingly.

Her uncle had told her mother that she had stepped out of pocket. He had basically told her that Stacy had got a spanking and all her mother had to do was follow through with grounding her, which lasted all weekend.

Stacy wondered why her uncle lied to her mother. Why was he protecting her, and what for? But she was more worried about talking to her friend about what had happened. She didn't know what, if anything, her uncle had said to Lisa. The only thing Stacy could do was talk to Lisa, for which she had to wait until Monday.

That was how Stacy got her first girlfriend at the age of nine. They avoided doing anything at Stacy's house as they didn't want to risk getting caught again. But every time Stacy went over to Lisa's, they ended the night with Stacy kissing all over Lisa's body.

"Just be still, okay?" Stacy would tell her girlfriend.

She knew if Lisa had liked everything so far, she would go crazy if she licked her pussy. Maybe? So, one night, after the usual kissing, Stacy continued down Lisa's stomach. Gently, she opened her legs.

"Nikki! What are you going to do?" Lisa asked, shocked.

"Do you want me to stop, Lisa?" Stacy asked.

"No!"

"Then don't be frightened," Stacy whispered.

She stuck out her tongue and licked Lisa's pussy. *Yuck,* she thought. It was salty. But Lisa had moaned. *Oh okay,* thought Stacy, *she likes it.*

She quivered inside. Stacy enjoyed the simple fact that Lisa liked it. Stacy never made those kinds of sounds she was used to hearing. *What is wrong with me?* She wondered. She opened Lisa's pussy lips and licked inside. *Oh my God, that is the worst!* But Lisa had begun to twitch and squirm.

Then quick as a rabbit, Lisa jumped up and ran out of the room with her hands between her legs. Stacy sat up, worried.

Did I bite her? She wondered as she waited for Lisa to come back to her room with her mother. Stacy expected the worst. She was nervous. She believed she had done something wrong.

When Lisa came back to the room, Stacy was so upset she didn't give Lisa any time to speak. "Damn it! I messed up, didn't I?"

"No, silly! I ran because I was about to pee on your face."

"What the fuck! I would have bit you then!"

They both laughed so loud, Lisa's mother, Ms. Angie, came into the room to tell the girls to be quiet.

"Why are you girls up?" She asked.

Lisa couldn't stop laughing. "Ma, I almost peed in the bed!"

"Oh, no. Did you?"

"Nah, I caught it just in the nick of time!"

"Lisa, no more juice before bed, okay?"

Stacy was surprised Lisa's mother had not asked any other questions. Though she enjoyed the time spent at Lisa's house, she was confused about how everything was done to her by her father that disgusted her, pleased Lisa when she did it to her. *Why?*

Stacy was confused; she didn't know what she really wanted in life. But she did know she was really attracted to Lisa. She also didn't know if her father ruined her, or if she was damaged.

Both girls were nine years old at the time it happened. They were each other's first female encounter. Stacy wondered why nobody asked her what was going on in her house. Was it because they knew it, or because they didn't want to know? It's a question Stacy will never know.

But Stacy knew she couldn't have a prolonged relationship with Lisa. She knew she would want to end with Lisa as she didn't want to do to someone what her father was doing to her almost every hellish night.

She didn't want to hurt her girlfriend… her best friend… her only friend. However, as much as Stacy's intentions were pure for Lisa, she did end up hurting her.

Chapter 5 - A Broken Family

Stacy froze. Her father was coming right at her for help. She didn't move. He zoomed past her, and she saw the knife sticking out of his upper back near his left shoulder blade. Did her mother stab her father? Yep, she did.

Stacy's father ran out the door, groaning and moaning. Those moans didn't sound like the ones she heard at night; *guess he didn't enjoy being penetrated either,* thought Stacy.

She walked into the kitchen and found her mother gathering more knives. When she spotted Stacy, she walked toward her calmly and said, "Nikki, I need you to pick up the phone and call the police. Tell them your mother said she wanted you to tell them that she's going to kill your father."

"911. How may I help you?"

"My mother told me to call you and say that she's going to kill my daddy."

"Do we need to send an ambulance along with the police?"

"I guess so. My dad does have a knife in his back."

Not too long after that, Stacy's mother was in the police car, and her father was in the ambulance, sitting on the edge of the patient's bed, getting his wound cleaned. A social worker watched Stacy until her grandparents came to pick her up. They had had her little sister since morning, so they were shocked by the development of events since their last visit the same day.

That night, after taking a bath and eating dinner, Stacey was tucked in bed by her grandmother.

"Nikki, what happens within a family stays within the family. So, I don't have to worry about you saying anything, right?" asked the grandmother.

"First, I have loyalty to my God, second to my children, and then my family," Stacy repeated her lesson.

"So, I am telling you to keep your mouth shut," the grandmother ordered.

That was a lot of pressure on Stacy. She realized she was alone.

She woke up her grandparents arguing with her father.

"Chris, have you lost your mind? She told the police you tried to take her toenails off with a pair of pliers."

"That woman is a lunatic, Ma. They won't believe her," Stacy's father boasted. "Plus, she has a history of crazy. If I'm not worrying, you shouldn't either."

"Also, I'm taking her to court for a divorce and full custody of the kids. I need you to back me up," he explained, "No judge in their right mind would give a schizophrenic custody. She proved it by running her husband through the neighborhood with several butcher knives."

He walked down the hallway with confidence toward his daughters.

"Kids, your mother had to go away for a while. But you don't have to worry."

"Will she be back soon?" Stacy asked.

"It's for the best. I'm doing this for your safety, okay?"

Yeah, right, my safety. Nobody cares about my safety, thought Stacy. She had been dealing with this BS for a long time, so she knew.

"Nikki, you need to be a big girl. You need to remember what happened in our home stays there. Damn it, if I find out you have been running your mouth about anything, I will come for you and beat that ass." He grabbed her by her arms. "Do you understand me, Nikki?"

"Yes, sir. I understand." Stacy said in a shy voice, nodding her head up and down.

"You've been warned." He spoke between clenched teeth.

Days passed with no sound from her father or mother. Stacy enjoyed the chance of living with her grandparents on their small farm. It kept her busy. Early mornings consisted of helping her grandfather with feeding the chickens and gathering their eggs. After that, it was time to wash and feed the hunting dogs and make slop for the hogs.

Her experiences with her grandparents were nurturing. No harm came to her. Weeks and months passed, and she began to feel different. Stacy was starting to feel happy inside, though she was scared. It was hard to let go and live.

And then, it happened.

Beep. Beep. "Hurry up, girls, we can't be late." Stacy heard a familiar voice coming from the yard.

"Our ride is here," her grandmother said.

Stacy knew they weren't going to the church, though it was Sunday. She walked to the car, and her father got out from the driver's side and opened the door for her. She couldn't move; she was frozen in place.

Why? was all she thought. She couldn't believe it.

"What's wrong with you?" Her father asked. "Get in the car, Nikki," he said as he pushed her inside.

Her stomach was upset during the drive. She didn't know if she wanted to puke or pass out.

"So, did you miss your daddy?"

"Yes! Are you coming to get us from grandma's house?" Stacy's sister was quick to answer and ask.

"Not yet. But you can come some weekends and stay with Dad. What do you think?"

"Yes. Yes. Yes. Yes. Yes," her little sister kept repeating excitedly.

"So, what do you think, Nikki? You want to come to see Daddy's new place?"

Choked up, she replied in a whisper, "I don't think I can. There's no one to help Grandpa on the farm. It's a lot of responsibility."

He looked at her from the rearview mirror. "Well, I'm the adult, and when I'm ready, I'm coming to get you. So be ready and no lip," he commanded.

"Yes, sir."

She knew she couldn't win against him.

They pulled up to the courthouse. Her grandmother and father turned around from the front seat. They lectured her on and on about not saying a thing. The grandmother talked about how helpful her father had been to the mother, how unbalanced she was, that they didn't know anything about the father putting his hands on the mother, and that it could be a figment of her imagination.

Stacy's father ended the talk, "If I hear you say anything other than what I told you, Nikki, you will regret it. If he doesn't ask you a question, don't volunteer any information."

"Order. Order in the court. All stands. You may be seated. Honorable Judge Albert Clements is here to bring judgment to the divorce of Christopher Thomas and Deana Thomas."

Stacy couldn't hear much else. She just felt like she sat there for a long time.

Next thing she knew, an officer named Bell asked her to follow him to the judge's chambers. It seemed to her as if she was in a museum. She felt as if it would take days to walk to the chair. She was glad the officer was beside her because if she fell, he could carry her the remainder of the way.

"Have a seat, Nikki. The judge will be in shortly."

Stacy thought the door sounded like it needed oil. It was odd because everything looked new to her, but she remembered looks can be deceiving.

The judge entered. He was a double-chinned, pudgy man with a red face. If Stacy was naïve, she would have thought him to be Santa Claus in hiding. He sat in the chair next to her and said, "Nikki, do you know why you are here?"

"Not really," she replied.

"Well, your mother and father want what's best for you. But you could only live with one."

"So, I'm here to help them figure that out? Do you know the best parent we should stay with?"

Stacy prayed the judge heard her heart because she wanted to be that naïve. He was Santa Claus. He knew what she wanted. She had been asking for it every year and hadn't received it yet.

"Sort of. What do you think?"

"I don't know."

"First, have you seen your father hurt your mother?"

She stayed quiet.

"The story with the knives, is that true?"

"Yes, sir." She could answer that one.

"I listened to the 911 call. It must have been scary for you. Were you scared, Nikki? What did you think will happen?"

"That my mama was going to kill my daddy." It was the truth, but not all of it.

"Did you see your dad try to pull off your mother's toenails?"

"No, I didn't see it."

He continued to question. Stacy felt it to be draining.

"What do you want from your parents, Nikki?"

She looked up at the judge and spoke in a low voice, "I wish they stop fighting." That was it.

41

"I wish they stop fighting." *What the fuck.*

She couldn't think of anything else to say.

The judge stood up and walked Stacy to the officer.

"Thank you, Nikki. I enjoyed our talk. If you have to choose, who would you like to live with?"

She answered without any hesitation. "Grandma, please. I don't want to go back with my father, and it seems my mother isn't a good option."

"Okay, Nikki. I understand."

She truly hoped he did.

Stacy felt defeated on the drive back. She hadn't seen her mother and had no clue how the evening was going to end. They arrived at grandma's house, and her father turned around to speak.

"Okay, you are going to stay with Grandma, and soon, every other weekend, I will come pick you up to stay with me to give Grandma a break."

Stacy couldn't believe her ears. She knew she didn't have to leave, so she felt encouraged. She decided to worry about those weekends when they arrived. At that time, she was happy. She jumped out of the car and ran inside the house to tell her grandpa the news.

"Grandpa, we're staying!" He was just as happy as she was.

Her grandmother came in with her crying sister, but Stacy couldn't care less. She had made the decision, and she was happy with it. She hoped everything would change for the better.

A few weeks passed, and she was settling into the change when she heard her grandma on the phone, "Okay, Chris. They'll be ready."

"For what?" She asked.

"You're going over to your dad's tomorrow."

Shit! It was too good to be true.

When wars and conflicts cease,

The world shall be at peace,

People will learn to get along,

And not blame others for being wrong.

They fight for control,

Because they want to continue to hold on.

If they could only see the harm they are causing, making an enemy of many.

Instead of fighting for humanity and reaching to embrace tranquility.

All we want in life is peace,

Someone to come home to,

Love and joy to spread and embrace,

A calm we can give to all.

Chapter 6 - Living with Grandparents

She had many moments of complete enjoyment during her childhood spent at her grandma's house. Since her sister was watched by her grandma most of the time, Stacy wasn't completely responsible for her sister anymore and felt more relaxed.

Her grandparents were a blast. Her grandfather, "King David" as his friends called him, was a truck-driving, hog-slopping, chicken feet, goat-eating, and rabbit-hunting fool. He was, and remained, all her heart. No one loved that man as much as Stacy did. To her, everything in the world revolved around him. He was her father.

They spent a lot of time together doing things like watching the Braves game. She would feed him his beer as if he were a baby wanting a pacifier and wash his back when he took a washup. See, her grandparents were old to the point that, at night, they all would take a tub of warm water and wash up. They didn't hop into the bathtub like normal folk, but they were country enough to just bathe up before bed.

By day, her grandfather was a manager at environmental services at the courthouse. Stacy couldn't wait until her grandfather got home. In the evenings, she would wait on the porch for him. Sometimes, he allowed her to accompany him to feed his hogs. She sat in the front seat of the truck and waved at everyone who would see her with him. She always had a huge smile on her face when she was with him.

The relationship between her grandparents was something very different than what she had been raised in, how it was between her parents. Though her grandparents didn't like each other, they did love each other. No matter what happened between them, they still took their evening walks together. If they had any arguments, Stacy and her sister never knew it.

That was the difference. When her parents fought, everyone knew it, even the newspaper. Stacy picked up the paper once and read an article stating her father had tried to remove her mother's toenails with pliers in one of their fights.

She also read in a newspaper that her mother was trying to get back their custody. She had a lawyer and was trying to prove abuse. It was very sad to read for Stacy. It was also shocking and embarrassing for her to go to school and have everyone know what happened to her family. She was asked more times than she could count, "Stacy, how is your mother?"

She thought *just because everyone knew it didn't mean they had to show her they knew it*. But that was how it was like in the little town she grew up in.

It made school very difficult for her. She had nobody to talk to about these things. But talking to her grandpa, or pawpaw as she called him, was still easier because he let her finish her sentences, unlike her grandma and mama. She got a pass from Stacy because her grandma, along with her grandpa, were raising two girls; that too in their sixties when all they had known about was raising boys. She believed they did a good job of raising her and her sister, better than her parents anyway.

Her mother had two brothers. The oldest was a true Johnny Cash idol, black cowboy hat and all, and her twin was a larger-than-life drunk and a ghost, meaning he wasn't around for long if he was even around in the first place. Stacy's mother also had two sisters. The older sister had a rock iron fist, and she was the aunt they, i.e., Stacy and her siblings, were disciplined by often.

Their first cousins were like sisters and brothers to them. They loved hanging out with their extended family all the time. Though Stacy could see her aunt help as much as she could, she also noticed that her aunt didn't really look hard enough.

Stacy's mother's younger sister was the kindest but showed favor to one sister than the other. To Stacy, she appeared to have an 'out of sight out of mind' attitude toward her mentally sick sister, since not one time did Stacy remembers her younger aunt asking about her mother or assisting Stacy and her siblings in any way. She lived somewhere else; and maybe that was a good excuse.

She made Stacy wonder if she was fighting away a few demons herself. They say mental illnesses, even depression, can be found within the family. Stacy can definitely see a pattern of suicides, depression, and underlying drug and alcohol abuse in her family and how similar patterns unfolded in her life. She found it sad that everyone struggled with it on their own, knowing everyone else was also struggling while pretending that everyone, including themselves, was fine. Secrets kept within families can rotten the core within.

Stacy's father was the middle of three boys. They all had their own special issues. Her older paternal uncle had a wife and two children. He would come over and hang out with her father often. They would drink, smoke, snort, hang out with girls, and party with neighbors.

Stacy knew that her uncle had seen, on several occasions, how her father treated her, but he never stepped in or helped her. She knew it was why she didn't get to go over to this uncle's house either, because Stacy knew too much, and her younger sister had no clue what was going on. She was naive and safe.

Stacy had the coolest bond with her cousin RayRay. They did nothing but laugh the entire time. They fueled each other's funny bone. Stacy never knew if her uncle's wife knew what was going on; her mouth was as tightly closed as Stacy's. What happens in the family stays in the family, right?

Later in life, one often finds out things that turn around their world and leave them in utter shock.

Her younger paternal uncle was known as "Feather" for his flamboyant nature. He ended every sentence with, "Ooh, please!" Everyone had a feeling he was a free spirit, but Stacy never got to know it for certain, not before he passed.

Stacy recalls her uncle telling her she was disgusting. He made it an unpleasant memory of himself to hold on to. He was the one who had caught Stacy with Lisa. He would do the weirdest thing: he would talk to Stacy, but in an unpleasant way, he would call her out, but when it came to her cousin RayRay, he showed so much love and kindness. All Stacy felt was disgust for her complexion. It wasn't a unique experience. She was called Blackie or Little Black Girl. As usual, she couldn't go

49

anywhere without being called Charcoal Bits, Tar Baby, Midnight, Blackout, and other such names. No safe place for Stacy.

It affected her more than she let on. To this day, Stacy still asks how she looks in certain colors.

Stacy's childhood experiences define how she governs herself as an adult. She watches people differently, but she doesn't allow that to prevent her from enjoying life. The impact of her negative experiences during her childhood has modeled Stacy, but she hasn't let it cripple her.

She developed an attitude of not letting anyone get close to her. Even today, she makes it impossible for anyone to find out anything about her or her family. If she wants you to know, she will share.

She shuts off from nonsense, or at least she tries. Yet she still wonders why she allows so much drama from the people in her life.

She wonders what was wrong with her, or still is, for her not to get the love she deserves. She makes it a point to express to everyone the feelings of love and appreciation she feels for them, yet it's so hard for her to earn them back. She just wishes to be shown the love that she shows from the people she shows it to. Even if others cannot express the way she does, she believes it would be great to just receive some love.

Sometimes, she wonders if she expects a lot from people. Maybe it is what will be her downfall.

Thinking about how she feels the way she does, it may be because of the attention, the right kind of it, that she never received from her father. She catches herself catering to others the way she wishes they would treat her. She sees them enjoy it, too. But they don't respond to her with the same warmth and fondness. Isn't it said that you should treat people the way you like to be treated? It is what they may say, but in Stacy's experience, not everyone abides by it.

Stacy catches herself feeling an overwhelming sense of love for others. She feels stupid for feeling that way. As time goes on, some changes do take place. But then something or the other unforeseen must happen and she finds herself standing at square one. Sometimes, she regrets being the way she is. She can still feel the negative effects that her father had on her life. Maybe it's because she still wishes he had a major, positive role in her life. She knows it cannot happen and will not happen. Even if it did happen, she probably wouldn't trust it.

Stacy's family wasn't affectionate, except for her mother. She was the best at making it known how she felt about her children. When she was in the right frame of mind and not hearing voices, she was funny and playful. She said, "Showing someone how you feel about them is the best and cheapest gift to give." It is because of her expression of love that made her feel less lonely, despite their differences.

Stacy's mother was so loving. She wasn't the most affectionate or nice of a person when she was mother dearest, but she never went a day without expressing her heart in some strange and crazy way. Stacy could see she tried to be a good mom, despite her mental illness. But being married to an alcohol and drug addict was intense for her and added to her mental health struggle. Stacy's mother's meat wasn't wrapped too tight inside her taco, and latterly, her father exploited that to his favor.

She became more and more ill as time went on. A time came when Stacy's mother couldn't tell reality from imagination. She was in and out of mental facilities. Stacy's father was still hitting her mother. At the time, he was in the process of getting a divorce. But to Stacy, it felt like he was giving up on the family he had created and destroyed.

Stacy's mother turned on her, because of the abuse he inflicted on both together. Stacy's mother saw his face instead of Stacy's. Doctors called it *Prosopometamorphopsia;* visual distortion or facial displacement is an easier terminology. So when she looked at Stacy but saw her father, she would start screaming uncontrollably and hitting her. Stacy would have to defend herself, sometimes even call the police.

Stacy remembered having to sit in front of the judge and describing how she felt. Her mom's family had said that her father was abusive. Stacy had witnessed it. She remembered thinking how she could tell the judge everything that went on in her home.

She sat in this big office, in front of this enormous white man, and he asked Stacy, "Darling, is there anything you want to tell me?" She opened her mouth, she had so much to say, but could only utter, "I wish we could be a family." That was all she could muster up to say to him.

Her mother screamed at the top of her lungs upon hearing that. Stacy and her sister were shipped to live with her paternal grandparents until her father was ready to be a father.

Her grandma never wanted to hear what went on at their home. She only said, "Everybody has problems at home." That was the end of it. From that point on, Stacy or her sister never talked about the relationship between their parents, nor did they talk about the visits they had with their father when he came to pick them up for the weekends, which was once in a blue moon anyway.

Stacy's life, from that point on, changed again. It was always important to her to have authentic love shown to her. Bonding was difficult growing up, when Stacy was younger, she didn't develop like most children. Stacy felt she had raised herself. She couldn't have a normal chance in life; she was too busy doing something for everyone else.

Stacy's father and grandmother were given joint custody. Stacy was just happy to spend more time with her grandfather. She missed her mother, but she knew she wouldn't be able to see her, let alone be with her ever again. Stacy's mother had received six years for attempted murder in a mental institution, but because she was schizophrenic, it wasn't prison.

Stacy hoped her mother would get treated and get better. Maybe she could be allowed to see her once she got out. Little did Stacy, or anyone else, know that being admitted to the mental institution was going to be the beginning of the downward slope for her mother's mental health.

It seemed to Stacy that her life was only getting more difficult. This feeling often made her feel as if she was continuing to go around in circles again, off track again. "Cut and Hide"

Chapter 7 - A Makeshift Family

Spending weekends with her father gave him the opportunity to restart the entire nightmare once again. Stacy had hopelessly wished that the whole ordeal had concluded. She learned that events come back but in different ways. Her strong-mindedness made her prepared for a new chapter. In a strange and twisted way, Stacy's father had her equipped for the unexpected.

Stacy lay there with her eyes closed, concentrating, listening to Tasha's moans in delight as she continued to lap her pussy. She was reminiscent of a dog lapping on its desired meal or beverage. She slid her left hand slowly up Stacy's stomach, seeking to reach her breast.

"How does it feel, Nikki? Aren't you enjoying how I'm pampering this pussy? Tell me what you want from me," Tasha begged.

"Either you do it without asking me questions or get your face out of my pussy. I'm getting sleepy, and I'm ready to turn over and go to sleep, damn it!" Stacy replied in a very irritated tone.

Taken aback by what she had just been said to her in a very rude way, Tasha got up and walked to the bathroom to brush her teeth. She was royally pissed off and shocked by the sudden outburst. But Stacy didn't really care.

For the past three weeks in a row, her father had picked her and her sister up. He wanted them to bond with him and his new, ready-made family. While he didn't make them call her mom, they weren't allowed to call her by name either. So, what the hell where they supposed to call her? To be on the safe side, Stacy didn't ask for a thing. She basically didn't speak unless spoken to. Even then, she simply said, "Yes or no, ma'am."

It was Stacy's opinion, though, that her father wanted them to call her mom, but she'd be damned if she ever called her that. She would never be her mother! Stacy had realized she didn't have to like her, nor address her. So, she didn't unless something was asked of her. Stacy somewhat knew it was a setup for a disaster; she could feel it.

Honestly, Stacy wasn't expecting her father to beat down his girlfriend's ass. She went on pure adrenaline high of the anticipation of a weekend smackdown. Fuck, Stacy and her mom deserved one; her father's girlfriend needed one as well. But as it turned out, they were informed that they had to get along with her daughters.

"Why?" Stacy asked.

"Oh, they will soon be your stepsisters." Her father simply replied.

Fucking wonderful.

"Nikki, you know that we've gotten close over these past few weeks. I don't understand why you're so outright mean to me. You have to remember that you made me fall for you." Tasha kept pleading with her emotions.

She reached out for her hand, but Stacy pulled away quickly.

"You can be such a bitch, Nikki," Tasha continued crying and wanting Stacy to reach out for her in comfort. "Why are you treating me this way, damn it? I wish I hadn't let you even touch me."

She was trying her best to get her point across to Stacy, but she just didn't have time for this nonsense.

"Shut up!" Stacy said tiredly. "We both have a choice in this, so if you are annoyed, I have a solution. We're done!"

"No!" She screamed in a hysterical panic. "I didn't say that. I just want you to be nicer to me, please. It's hard to handle your swinging attitude toward me. Nikki, it bothers me how one day we were laughing, playing, and enjoying each other's company. Then, like a switch, you become distant and hateful to me. Hot then cold, up and down like a roller coaster. It's important to me for you to believe me when I tell you I really like you a lot."

Tasha went on talking throughout the night until Stacy finally said what she wanted to hear.

"Okay, I will do my best."

Her mother had always told her never to say, "I'll try." She remembered her mother saying, "Sweetie, my mother said, trying is like the phrase, 'I'll see.' When you're ready, it will be because you are ready, not because someone begged you. When you want to do something, you will attempt to do your best, and it shows that you're considering their feelings."

Tasha and Stacy had hit it off the first weekend she visited with her dad. But that was only because Tasha hated the fact that her mother was dating Stacy's dad.

Stacy had stayed outside on the swings in the playground. Later, Tasha came up and sat beside her. They started to talk and realized how familiar their attitudes were with their parents' dating situation. Plus, sleeping in the same room and bed together increased their friendship level.

The two eldest shared one room, while the two youngest shared the other.

They were playing twisters one night in their room, laughing and enjoying themselves. With the right hand on blue and the left foot on green, suddenly Stacy fell on top of Tasha as her left hand slipped to yellow. They both burst out laughing.

It was then that Stacy wanted to see how Tasha would react to her giving her a kiss. As it turned out, she was expecting her lips and then her hot tongue.

"Oh shit, you're such a good kisser. Who taught you?"

Yeah, like I'm going to tell you. Stacy thought to herself. *Hell no.*

Ignoring her question, she kept the kiss going. Getting up, she told Tasha forcefully, "Get that ass in the bed."

It came as a surprise how she enjoyed ordering Tasha around. Still standing at the light switch, she belted out, "Take off your clothes, and I mean down to your bare essentials."

She lay there naked, like a skinned chicken. Stacy knew full well what she was doing, but something compelled her to give in to the sexual arousal. She lay next to her in bed, naked. The tip of her right index finger glided down Tasha's body, causing her to whimper and moan in pleasantries. While touching her all over her body, she lightly traced the same areas with her tongue, causing her to call Stacy's name.

"Oh shit, Nikki."

Rubbing and pulling on her hard nipples, she could feel herself enjoying every unusual action. She slowly caressed and kissed down to her pussy. Moaning and squirming underneath her, Tasha was enjoying her techniques. The techniques her father had practiced with her. The techniques her father had practiced with her, she was inflicting on someone else, and it didn't faze her at all.

It was just so odd how anyone could enjoy this act. Yet here she was doing something that repulsed her.

Tasha got louder and louder, and Stacy knew she was about to burst because her every word was, "Nikki, Nikki."

"Okay, now enough with the noise. It's annoying me, Tasha."

"But it feels so good. I can't believe it."

Stacy couldn't believe it either, that she was doing this again.

"The way you move your tongue around my pussy. It's driving me insane," she said between grunts and moans. "You're going to make me erupt all in your mouth."

Stacy continued to maneuver her index finger in her wet pussy back and forth, slowly feeling her walls clench her finger tight. Tasha continued to fuck her finger and asked her to go deeper and faster. Stacy slid a second finger into her pussy, and she gave out a loud moan. Stacy knew she had come.

Pulling her fingers out, Stacy placed her clear-coated, milky, creamed fingers toward her face and demanded that she lick them.

Without hesitation, she barked out the same command again, "Suck them, now!"

Tasha opened her mouth, and she guided her finger into her hot mouth.

"Now that's more like it. Don't let me ever have to repeat myself, ya' hear?

"Okay," Tasha replied quickly.

Stacy got up and went to the bathroom to clean herself up. When she arrived back, Tasha stared at her strangely. She then got up and headed to the bathroom as well.

When she came back, Stacy had her pj's on and was facing away from the door to get some sleep.

"Nikki, can we talk?"

"No. Go to sleep, and don't utter a word about this to me. It's not up for discussion," she bellowed.

Tasha got into the bed and tried to place an arm around her, but Stacy stopped her in the mid-lift of her arm.

"Don't touch me. Don't ever touch me unless I say you can."

Quickly, she turned, and that was their first night together.

From the very beginning, it can be said that Stacy was a challenge. But now Tasha was asking her to change. Whenever she tried to ignite sex, Stacy would say, "I don't feel like fucking with you right now, Tasha."

If it was reversed and Stacy felt frisky, there was no denying her of what she wanted. Their relationship was entirely one sided, Stacy's side. She called all the shots, and she wouldn't hesitate to end it if there was any friction. It was what her father liked, control and authority. Sadly enough, she liked it as well.

Stacy's summer with her father and his new family was interesting. Her attitude was coarse for a young teen.

Her father never disciplined nor scolded her for having a foul mouth. He considered it a way of "self-expression."

If she didn't curse at an adult or show disrespect toward her grandparents, everything would be fine. If she did, she expected a beating.

So, Stacy made it a point to express herself often, particularly when Bard was around. She hated it, which meant Stacy enjoyed it. But she never said anything in return, so she knew her father had that ass under control as well.

One rainy day, Tasha and Stacy were in their room, watching television. She was getting quite needy.

"You suck, you know? I can't stand this shit. You never hug me or give me compliments. Why?"

"Tasha, I really don't want to deal with this crap today, okay?"

Still yapping at the mouth, Stacy got up and walked out of the room. She knew Tasha wouldn't follow her. This was something they argued about in private. She was completely paranoid about her mother finding out what was going on between them.

Slam. Stacy shut the door so hard the shaking of the handle could be heard throughout the house. That made Barb come around the corner to see what was going on upstairs.

Tasha opened the door and yelled, "You're so hateful, Nikki." With that, she slammed the door shut.

Pissed off, Stacy reopened the door and cursed at her, "You needy bitch. Watch what you're saying now. Check your shit because your ass will pay later."

As usual, once this was over, she would try to apologize and beg Stacy to fix it. Whatever *it* was, hell, if she knew. Shutting the door again and heading downstairs, she came across Barb, who was standing in awe of her behavior and language toward her daughter.

Honestly, Stacy didn't give two flying fucks about her daughter. She really didn't care. All she had was complete hatred toward her daughter, Barb, herself, her life, and her motherfucking father. She just didn't give a damn. "Cut and Hide"

She tried getting past Barb, but she stopped her and said, "I think you need to apologize to your sister."

Stacy shot her a look so evil she stepped back.

"Who? Tasha? She's not my sister. She's just needy." Stacy stated simply. "You're needy too. I'm so sick of needy bitches." Her words made Barb gasp.

Stacy proceeded to walk past her. She flicked on the television and sat on the couch, waiting for her father. She knew either she would get smacked in the face or worse. Worse being a pussy check.

A pussy check was just what it sounded like. He would say, "So, you've grown, huh? So, you're smelling yourself now? You've got the puffy chest, your shit's so bad, you're bold, huh? Let me show you who's running things in this house."

He would take her to the bathroom and tell her to pull down all her clothes and penetrate his finger in her pussy. Humiliating and demeaning her in every way. This was frequently done to bring Stacy off her "high horse." A reality check to show her he was still in control.

"Lick it," he would command, placing his fingers in her mouth.

So, she sat and waited for her punishment without any fear. She could care less because he would always find a reason to give her a pussy check anyway.

Fuck it.

Two hours later, the sound of a car door being closed in the carport could be heard. Like a little child, Barb was waiting for his return. She quickly ran out the door to confront him about what Stacy had done that evening.

"Chris, you wouldn't believe what Nikki said to Tasha and me."

"What?"

"She's so rude, and her attitude is so unpleasant."

"Dammit, Barb, tell me already," he rushed. "You're beating around the bush. What the fuck did the little black say?"

Her father would become irritated so fast; Stacy knew she got that trait, plus a lot more, from him. She knew he was getting pissed. Damn it, she knew from the slamming of the car door. After years of cowering in the quiet and studying his moods, she knew when he was in a bad one.

The best way to know or defeat an enemy or opponent is to study, practice, and learn their habits. Something her father told her often. So, she tried never to get caught slipping in any situation.

"Chris, she said that we were needy bitches, and that Tasha should check her shit because she would check her ass later. Can you believe that mess? She really has a temper."

He glared at Stacy, who was sitting on the couch, watching television, with a blank look on her face.

She didn't move or look up.

As bold as she appeared, she could never look him in the face. She didn't even know if she ever looked her father in the eyes. It scared her.

"Chris! Did you hear me?" Barb nagged.

"Yes, damn it! I heard you already."

"So?"

"So, what, Barb? If you think about it, you both are needy as hell," he said abruptly. "I will handle it; go to your room."

Shocked by his tone, she turned and walked up the stairs obediently like a child. That was some freaky shit. But a grown-ass woman following the directions barked at her was normal to Stacy. She knew she had some sense not to go against her dad.

Judging by her reaction to his tone, she knew Barb had her ass checked by him a few times as well.

"The proof was in the pudding," quoting her grandma. Stacy smiled a little inside as she heard her run up the stairs.

She would be able to take the punishment now because she knew that Barb's home wasn't happy. She felt better knowing that it wasn't just her mother who got the sense knocked out of her. Her dad had turned Barb into a fruitcake as well.

Walking into the kitchen, she knew he was getting a pony. A small draft beer that could fit in the palm of your hand. He sat down beside her and handed her a drink. She was shocked, to say the least, but she didn't show it. They sat there for hours watching the football game— chilling, tripping, and screaming throughout the game.

Stacy didn't know how to express the feelings she experienced that day. Perhaps a better way to put it would be that Stacy enjoyed a stress-less moment with her father that Saturday.

When it was time for bed, he only said, "Know your place, Nikki. You don't pay the bills in anyone's house. So, check that attitude with adults, alright?"

"Yes, sir," she responded quickly.

"Tomorrow's another day, so fix it with an apology to Barb," he demanded. "I know you will figure out a way to work things out with your sister, Tasha. So, deal with that as well, you hear?"

"Yes, sir."

"Goodnight, black."

"Goodnight," she said, walking off, thinking he had her twisted if he thought she would ever apologize to Tasha. She wasn't worried because she knew it was squashed.

Stacy had been absent from the room the entire day, so she knew Tasha felt isolated since she never came downstairs. Being the needy person she was, she would want some attention from her.

She knew full well that Tasha would be the one to apologize. As Stacy walked up the stairs, she felt a rush of power. She was Billy badass with her chest puffed up. She knew she had an attitude, but that didn't bother her the least.

She deserved the right to carry the chip. No one had a clue how she felt, nor did they sit down to ask her what her problem was.

If Tasha pleaded for forgiveness, well, in that case, Stacy would let her eat her pussy that night. *Maybe,* she thought with a grimace on her face.

She studied the look and attitude Tasha displayed.

Stacy persisted in taking her hatred out on herself with self-mutilation, alcohol abuse, and self-isolation, all because of her father.

It gave her a violent energy, leading her to express her feelings through violent acts on others. She knew it wasn't healthy, but she didn't know how to express everything that she had felt for a very long time.

As she grew older, her therapists told her that continuous hatred may lead to a desire for revenge or sporadic outbursts, which she often had. She stopped acting on the violent feelings and took to writing all that she was carrying inside of her.

Chapter 8 - The Plan

Several weeks passed before Stacy returned to her father's place. She didn't know if it was punishment or because Barb was spending time with her family in the South.

During the time Stacy did not visit her father, Barb often called her grandmother and asked if she could pick her sister up to spend the day with them. Her grandmother didn't seem to mind. She would only have Stacy to deal with, and with her already being fourteen years old, she wasn't a bother. Stacy never inquired about their outings or asked to go along.

Besides, she loved spending time with her grandparents. They lived in a modest double-wide trailer surrounded by animals on their property. No one bothered her there unless she wanted to be bothered. She found it calming. Everything there was peaceful for her, be it helping them out with daily chores or spending time with her grandfather. In fact, some of the best moments of her life were the time she spent with her grandfather.

Nikki savored her time with Aaron. He lived up the street from her grandparents, was a junior from another school, and told her often that she seemed older than a sophomore in high school. Since they didn't go to the same school, there wasn't any crowding in each other's personal space, which allowed their friendship to be more fun.

They had met while Stacy was over at her cousin's house one evening after church. They hit it off effortlessly. That was the easy part. She could talk to Aaron for hours but couldn't tell him everything about her life because she didn't know how he would react.

Aaron had already started asking her questions about her reasons for not wanting to visit her father. Whenever he did, she felt it would be best to change the subject. Although he knew a few things about her father, and that her mother had some medical issues: but nothing more.

They would see each other at the church and visit each other's place on a frequent basis. Stacy enjoyed his company, and she could tell he felt the same. He was a gentleman toward her, mainly because he never brought up sex. He had high morals for himself and her. They commonality was music and laughter continuously.

While they were attracted to each other, building a friendship was more important than sex, and thus it was the furthest thing from his or her mind. Because once it fades, the only thing one is left with is friendship. He became her haven when she least expected it. Their friendship meant a lot to her, and it coming to an end would be heart-wrenching and devastating.

They traveled to a lot of places she wouldn't have expected to see around their city and county otherwise. They laughed all the time and had thoughtful and exciting conversations.

Aaron kept things light and interesting. He was easygoing, and his company was a pleasure. But most of all, he was calming to her spirit. She loved his family as well. It was something she wished she had grown up into a functional family. If they had any issues, it didn't show. Theirs was a family that meshed well.

Aaron also had a younger sister, which was convenient because whenever Stacy visited him, her little sister had to follow. Her father always reminded her that she had to watch over her sister. So, if she got into any trouble, it was going to be on Stacy. In a way, she was her sister's keeper, which was quite challenging quite often. *More pressures.* Cut and Hide.

But Aaron was a motivation in her life; he pushed her to continue to stay positive regardless of what she had going on. That's what made her care so much about him.

Yet, whenever she had to be around her father, no anxiety or pressure she felt was normal. Spending time around her father or simply knowing she had to, triggered a massive anxiety attack. Her attitude would change for the worse every time, and no one ever asked her why, which made her angry even more; not being understood. She just knew she was angry; she turned into a hellion.

Cut and Hide.

She sat on the porch, in a daze, fuming and thinking about having to go to her dad's for the weekend.

Cut and Hide.

"Lie Hue," her grandfather yelled, calling for her. That was the nickname he had for her.

She wasn't sure why, so she asked, "Pawpaw, why do you call me Lie Hue?"

"Because you're a liar. You lie about your feelings, and you lie to people as well," he responded straight to her face.

Uh-oh, she thought, shocked.

"You carry a dark cloud everywhere, Nikki. So, do you get it, a clouded lie? Lie Hue."

"Yes, sir."

They both smiled.

Her Pawpaw continued, "When you sit alone on the porch staring out into space, I ask you how you are and you always say, 'I'm great.' That's a lie. I've caught you lost in space often, sweetie. I know something is going on, and when you're ready, I'm here."

She wanted to open up to her grandfather, but she couldn't. She didn't know how to, rather she didn't know how he would react to what had been done to her, and what was happening now with Tasha. She was ashamed and embarrassed. She didn't want to disappoint him.

Tears ran down her face. He grabbed Stacy in his arms to comfort her, but she jerked because she didn't know how else to react.

Truly, she wasn't the hugging type. She didn't like anyone touching her unless she initiated it; rarely did she express affection.

But her Pawpaw continued to hold her. Stacy let her tears flow. Once he let go of the hug, her grandfather grabbed her face tight and said, "You are loved. And Pawpaw is here when you're ready to talk."

"Okay," was all Stacy could say, after which she walked away. Stacy left the house to visit her father without saying goodbye to her Pawpaw.

"Nikki," her little sister said.

"Yeah," she replied.

"Can you be nice to Barb?" She asked. "She says you don't like her, and she wants you to like her so much."

"Why?"

"She says that you make Daddy mean when you visit. You bring the whole weekend down for the family. So, will you be nice for once?" Her sister begged.

"Oh, really?" Stacy replied in a devious tone. She was shocked, to say the least, but it wasn't enough to deter her.

It's on, she thought. *Silent treatment, check. Attitude, check. Foul mouth, check. Poker face, check. Chips on both shoulders, check and check*; she was ready to go. Bitch was on the wheels this weekend. It would be her last time in that motherfucker's watch.

"How have you been? Have you been behaving for your grandparents? Is everything good? Do you need anything? If so, let me know before you leave this weekend." Barb had a lot to say.

Yeah, right, she thought. She wasn't about to give a response unless asked directly.

They watched television, ate chips, and continued with the fake-ass family skit until Stacy excused herself from everyone to go to bed. She knew if she went before Tasha, she could skip talking to her.

Tasha knew better than to touch or bother her when she was asleep. She knew better, even if Stacy faked it.

It had been a month since they had seen or been with each other. Stacy knew Tasha was dying inside for attention. *Nope, not tonight, needy,* Stacy laughed to herself.

The next morning, she woke up to Barb yelling, "Breakfast."

Stacy stretched and turned around in bed. Tasha was there, still lying next to her in the bed and staring stupidly at her.

"Did you miss me? I tried to get Mama to pick you up when we got your sister. She just said, 'next time.' I kept asking her why she wouldn't let you come, and she said it was because you're disrespectful."

Stacy stared at Tasha like she was crazy, which she was. She continued to look for a few moments, then got up and started to get dressed.

"Nikki, you know you are rude sometimes, right?" Tasha asked.

"Yes, I know I have my moments," she replied.

Stacy continued to explain herself to her because she knew this weekend would be her last one. Yep! She had a plan in the works that would end her suffering.

"Tasha, I'm complicated, and I like it when I distance myself from people. It's easier for me, really. I don't like drama, but it's necessary," she tried to explain. "I don't care if I'm hard to get close to. Understand?"

She looked at Stacy and said, "But I understand, Nikki. You're fun to be around. I really enjoy your company a lot. When we're alone, you're so funny and nice. I wish you showed that side of you more to everybody else."

Stacy knew Tasha liked her, and she didn't think she was too bad either. She almost felt bad for what she was going to do to her. But not really. She needed out, and Tasha was going to be collateral damage.

She grabbed her tight and started to kiss her deeply. She could have sucked her face off, all while laughing inside.

"When our parents go to the store, let's stay home and fuck, okay?" She whispered.

Tasha illuminated from the inside out. "Heck, yeah!" She yelped because Stacy had grabbed her ass.

It was on!

"Come eat, girls!" Barb yelled again.

Breakfast was typical. Catina, Tasha's younger sister, fussed about the last piece of bacon. Her father got his food served by the television as if he was too good to eat with everyone else at the table. Stacy couldn't care less. She just wanted to end that weekend disaster.

"Okay, go get ready for the day so we can go to the store," Barb said. She didn't have to say a thing. Quick as a rabbit, Tasha jumped in.

"Nikki and I want to go play outside since we haven't seen each other in a while. Please, mom?"

Stacy just stood there finishing her food, not reacting to Tasha's outburst.

"Sure, sweetie, I know you've been asking about her, so I know she missed you as well. Isn't that right, Nikki?"

"Yes, ma'am," she said hesitantly, not acknowledging Barb at all.

Barb hated it when Stacy disrespected her like that. But she didn't care; she was going all out for her master plan.

"Nikki, I wish you'd speak more," she said. "You make me think you don't enjoy coming over. I know your dad wishes you did, sweetie."

She stood up from the table slowly and politely said, "Barb (yes, she called her by her name), you don't have to speak for my father. He's in the living room. I know he's glad I'm here because he picked me up and brought me here." With that, Stacy started to walk away.

"Nikki, don't disrespect me again by using my first name. We have been a family for a long time, and you know that's not allowed, okay?"

"Sure, don't call me sweetie then," she responded, looking her straight in the eye.

As she walked away, she heard Barb walking behind her, moving toward the living room and glancing at her dad. He didn't say anything as she walked up the stairs.

She stopped to hear Barb whisper to him, "You're not going to say anything, Chris?"

"You know she's just like her father, quick-tempered. That's why she stays quiet because she does snap. So, don't fuck with her, Barb. I don't," her father snapped.

"You don't even try to help the situation, Chris. Why!"

She could hear her dad stand up from the couch. And then there was silence. Stacy knew who won that argument. She was smiling ear to ear, going into the room.

Phase one down, on to the next act.

While taking her shower, Stacy was deep in thought, thinking how she just knew that once that day was over, she would feel so content.

Regardless of the mess she was about to create, it didn't bother her. Being near her father made her feel so much like she didn't have control. She couldn't deal emotionally.

Even though she was fifteen years old, she still felt afraid, like a five-year-old too scared to sleep.

Once she dozed off, he would come into her room for some fatherly affection.

She needed to regain some control in her life, even if it was just from her father's visits. She finally understood what her grandfather was talking about before she left. There was something wrong. But she would only be able to solve it if she opened up to someone.

It was all too much. And it showed in her attitude toward people, life, and mainly herself. She wore her feelings on her shoulders, but no one knew the problem.

She wouldn't allow anyone the chance to get close enough to her. She was self-destructing. But she knew she had, at least, a chance of finding normalcy if she ended whatever she was doing with Tasha and just tried to open up to Aaron. She deserved the chance to try without any distraction from "father knows best."

She was standing in the shower, enjoying the warmth of the water on her body, and then suddenly, Tasha burst into the bathroom.

Pulling back the shower curtain and exposing all her nakedness, she yelled, "Hey, how long are you going to stay in there, Nikki? I would like to wash my ass as well."

Stacy hated it when she did that shit without knocking on the door. It was so rude and irritating.

She was frozen in mid-sentence, staring at her wash herself.

"What, Tasha? You're making me cold with the door and shower curtain open. Can I help you?"

But she didn't reply. Stacy knew what would get her to speak up, so she said, "I'm getting pissed."

Tasha quickly closed the door and started to strip to nothing.

"Get in," Stacy ordered. "You've been thinking of me getting that pussy, huh?"

She grabbed Tasha around the waist and proceeded to kiss her deeply.

"I love it when you kiss me, Nikki. It sends waves throughout my body. I wish you could stay with me. You can be the most gratifying person. If you want to spend more time with me, all you would have to do is get your attitude under check. Then you know my mom wouldn't mind picking you up like she does your younger sister. Catina and Lily get along well. Why can't we?"

"Tasha, shut up, please! You're turning me off."

Bringing up how their living arrangements should be and how she should act wasn't on her mind. She had one agenda, and making them all into one big happy, dysfunctional family wasn't it.

Rubbing all over her smooth body and kissing and sucking on her nipples simultaneously was pushing Tasha over the edge. Taking the time to kiss her neck gently, Stacy gently asked, "Have our parents left?"

Unable to take a breath, Tasha finally managed to utter a single word, "Yes!"

Getting out of the shower, she wrapped them both in a towel and headed for the room. Laying down on the bed, Stacy focused on her inner thighs.

Kissing and nibbling on and around her inner thigh area and pussy made her yelp with pleasure. She was begging her not to stop.

She wanted to prolong Tasha's upcoming release, so she gently kissed upward from her abdomen, outlining her stomach with her tongue. She clenched her tits again with her mouth.

"Grab that ass, Nikki. Oh, how I love the way you touch my body. I want to tell you so bad that I love you, but I know how you are about me emotionally expressing my feelings. I'm just going to say you really turn my knobs."

Stacy knew how she felt, but she couldn't really listen to her words. Her mind was concentrating on the sound of their parents coming home. She had to stick to the main goal here.

As much as she was going to miss her, she had a bigger goal at hand to play out.

Stacy continued sucking on her pussy in a gentle but very sexual way. She knew Tasha wanted to explode, but it had to be at the right time, or it wouldn't work out the way she had planned it.

Thank God she finally heard the car door closing and the garage door opening. Stacy knew it was the moment she could end Tasha's delight and her own unfortunate fate of demise from her father's new home.

She went for the ultimate sound that would bring them up the stairs. She licked the two dominant fingers of her right hand and inserted them into her hot, wanting pussy. Tasha yelled with delight as her orgasm erupted.

Stacy could hear their parents telling their siblings to stay where they were and rushing up the stairs in a hurry. They stopped at the door but didn't enter.

They were probably trying to figure out who was in the room. Just at that time, Tasha gave a willing scream of delight. Stacy lay there with her face between her legs while she grabbed her hair and head to contain her on her clit.

Suddenly, the door to their room was swung open by her father.

"What the fuck is going on here?"

They both looked up and saw their parents standing in complete shock. Tasha's mother screamed at the top of her lungs at the sight of Stacy's head between her daughter's thighs. Stacy knew all hell was about to be showered upon them both, though in which direction, she had no clue.

She just jumped up and waited for the collateral damage to appear. When she planned for this scene to happen, she hadn't thought it all the way through. She realized that her follow-throughs had been coming up short lately. This was becoming a recent issue with her, but she knew she was getting it under control.

Speaking her mind without thinking, weighing the consequences the right way, and gathering the right odds, she was dealing with everything without getting into a lot of trouble with her grandparents, or so she hoped.

This was going to be a tough one, though. She just knew that she had to choose her words carefully when talking to her father when he took her home.

Laying there still naked, she wasn't embarrassed at all. Why?

The naked body wasn't something that ashamed her. That was the result of many years of practice from her father. She knew this for a fact.

He sent Barbara out early in the morning with everyone except Stacy. "Errands," or so Tasha stated.

Yeah, right!

She knew it was "father-daughter time," of course. He was pissed since last night. Barbara had been nagging him all damn day and night since Stacy hadn't spoken to her when she got in the car on Friday. She couldn't stand it when she didn't get any respect.

"Take off everything, and don't leave anything on. I want you standing in front of me, black bare booty ass naked, damn it. I'm fucking tired of you coming to my goddamn house thinking you rule shit over here. I'm gonna show your black ass who runs shit in this house, BITCH! I don't understand, Nikki, why you have to make things so hard for me. When I do show you respect, give you your freedom, your space, what do I get? Lip, Nikki, that's it! Lip every Damn time.

I must listen to Barbara ask me why I allow you to escape punishment. Do you know why? Because I think you will enjoy my time with you. I think this is something you really miss. I have stopped enjoying our father-daughter moments because I really think this is something you are doing with me."

Smack. Stacy stumbled to the floor fast. Buck, bare-ass and all. She just knew this was not going to be naked.

She didn't want to get hit in the chest, so she made it a point to stay turned to the side. He had made it a point of humiliating her naked, and it was his go-to tactic. Always.

She knew this was going to be her last visit to that fucking house. A part of her beamed with joy, though she made sure to keep this happiness hidden.

Stacy knew she had made things difficult for Tasha, and she felt guilty for it. She knew she had basically sacrificed Tasha as her scapegoat.

It hadn't been easy. True, Stacy did not reciprocate the feelings Tasha had for her, but she had some sympathy for the poor girl, especially because of her mother. Stacy had a smidge of sympathy for Barb. Stacy knew Barb had placed herself into a relatively emotionally abusive relationship with her father as well.

Stacy only regretted that she had to leave Tasha with this horrible man. Stacy wished she could undo the damage she knew she was going to unleash onto this oblivious family and the hurt on Tasha.

Stacy and Nikki could only say, "May the glory of the Lord endure forever within their hearts."

Chapter 9 - An Explanation

It felt amazing to rub her fingers down Tameka's body. The idea completely overthrew her senses. She moved with every kiss, every touch underneath her trembling body. Stacy knew Tameka felt the wetness of her tongue slowly outlining her abdomen. Stacy gently guided down her index finger to Tameka's pussy, causing her to shriek with acceptance. The pleasure of tasting her delight made Stacy wet. Damn! She wanted it in her mouth.

Stacy opened Tameka's thighs and placed her head gently between them. Her mouth and nose were wide open for taste and aroma. Tameka stirred underneath her, but Stacy held her in place with both her arms entwined around her thighs, secured in place. She licked both sides of her pussy lips with the summit of her tongue while gently flicking her clit. Tameka went mad from the sensation.

Stacy came up just when she knew they were both about to explode. They entangled their legs in the scissor position, hot wet pussy to pussy. They were ready. They had been ready for the torture of sexual arousal to stop.

They grasped onto each other's legs for dear life.

Grunting and grinding, humping back and forth with force. Feeling the peak of their awaited orgasms. The sound of both of them squealing and panting.

"Oh my God. It's right there, Nikki."

"I know, Tameka. I know."

Every nerve in Stacy's ass and pussy was tingling. Damn it! She was about to burst. She knew either she or both were about to piss the bed.

"Nikki! Nikki!" Tameka screamed.

Stacy knew Tameka was going to beat her. If it's not just right, the noise level or concentration on the task at hand can make her lose the whole moment.

"Shut up!" Stacy grunted.

She wanted to erupt as well. But it seemed to her Tameka was going to fuck up her mood. *Concentrate*, she told herself.

"Nikki, please!" Tameka screamed. "Look! Damn it!"

Stacy opened her eyes, and there stood Vince, her husband. Shocked, but Vince just wanted an explanation.

Stacy had tried talking to Vince, but she knew he wouldn't understand, basically from all the other conversations she's tried to have with him that didn't get anywhere but through death ears.

"Everything is so bottled up inside of me. I don't know how to tell you what's in my heart. You won't understand me. You want to feel my soul inspiration, but the whole reason I feel I brought you into my life was to somewhat feel normal and stable or to prove my father wrong that someone could fall in love with someone like me, but not completely. I don't really trust you with the real me. To be honest, I don't even want to be alone in my own thoughts."

He looked at her dumbfounded.

"Why even be with me then?" he asked.

"Your sexuality made me feel comfortable, at least, feel comfortable in mine. That's the commonality we both shared." Stacy shrugged and added, "That's it, mainly. Fucked up, huh?"

Of course, things were never the same between Stacy and Vince from that point onward.

Chapter 10 - Blemished Perceptions

Growing up, a lot of us get hammered into our brains by our elders that if we treat people well, we will be treated the same way. Unfortunately, life teaches us otherwise.

Realistically, nobody is obliged to behave in a certain way with others. Nobody owes kindness, sympathy, or generosity to anybody. Some idealize being kind and respectful to others so much that they forget to treat themselves the same way. Others perceive the values but don't act on them.

Perception is defined as the process of acquiring, interpreting, selecting, and organizing information. It helps in figuring out what needs to be done. But if what needs to be done isn't done, perception is useless. In simple words, perception without action is pointless.

Perceptions, based on the teachings of others, not life, can often be wrong. This happens because, without experience, the difference between perception and reality cannot be understood.

Reality is the state of things as they are, as they exist. Perception is only a limited view and understanding of it. As we mature, our theories of reality and perceptions play a dominant role in how we live our lives. Our perception of our reality begins to define how we interact with it and the actions and reactions we exercise.

According to Stacy, her perceptions were flawed from her early life. Realistically, for as long as she can remember, she was damaged.

The basis of her belief in her brokenness stems from how she reacted toward her life. The core emotion that defined her perceptions of her life as a young woman was feeling unloved. There was something weird about her perceptions at that age, including her view of who she was earlier and at that age.

As a young woman, she was completely incapable of remembering the experiences in her past that had shaped her perceptions. She did not know what had happened. Evidence showed her perception was unreliable because her father was supposed to love her unconditionally.

But her perceptions were blemished, and her reality had been made to be seen as undependable and soiled by many people. How does an introvert have an extroverted disposition? It comes from having a messed-up way of living, along with being screwed, getting banged, and fucking with a lot of people along the way.

Chapter 11 - "It's Coming to an End"

Lights. Camera. Action. Now, quiet, everyone.

Roll it.

An outcry of claps and whistles filled the air surrounding Stacy. *Breathe, damn it! Breathe. Slow down and breathe before you pass out. Get yourself together.*

Spinning uncontrollably, she looked down at her feet to see if she was still stationary. Yes, she hadn't moved as she was waiting for the next scene.

Fade to black. Stacy passed out.

She sat in a wooden rocking chair, waiting. She could see the little girl, but she knew she was very young by her size in the chair. As she walked toward her, she recognized she was in a courthouse. She looked down at the floors and they shone so brightly. She didn't see herself mirrored in them, but the image of a young girl with tears running down her face. It was a scene from her early life.

Stacy sat in the living room watching television one Saturday evening. She couldn't really concentrate on whatever played in front of her. Her mind roamed through the events of the past few nights.

"Shh. Don't say a word," her mother whispered to her.

"Huh?" Stacy was confused.

"God came to me and told me you are suffering. I know, Stacy. I know everything. You couldn't come to me and I'm sorry."

Stacy began to cry. She didn't blame her mother, at least not entirely.

"It's coming to an end," her mother continued.

Stacy wondered what her mother was talking about. She didn't know if her mother was talking about what her father did to her or if she had gone completely batshit off her rocker.

After that day, Stacy's mother visited her room almost every night, saying the same thing. Stacy didn't know how to react to it since she didn't know what her mother was talking about, yet she couldn't wait. She wanted it, whatever it may be and whatever it was bringing an end to.

One night, the door opened as usual. *Here she comes again*, thought Stacy. But as soon as she heard the raspy voice, she knew she was wrong. It wasn't her mother.

"Take off your panties," the raspy voice told her.

Stacy zoned out. This was the only way she knew how to survive the ordeal. She stared at the pitch-black ceiling as he licked and lapped like a big dog. She hated the sounds he made as much as she hated his visits.

Stacy was distracted from her dissociation as she felt his fingers penetrating her. She was convinced he would pull out her intestines.

Maybe if I just close my…

Smack! "Stop trying to close your legs, dammit! Young girls don't start their periods at nine years old. I need to check if you are still a virgin." He argued.

Stacy wondered if her starting her cycle was the real reason behind him putting his fingers inside her.

A week ago, on a hot afternoon, Stacy was riding her bike at an uncontrollably fast speed while going downhill. It caused the bicycle chain to pop off. Stacy had no choice but to use her feet to bring the bicycle to a stop. But as she tried to stop going down the slope, she slipped. Her vagina hit the inner bike bar.

Stacy came home running to tell her mother what

had happened so she could check if she was alright. Her mother pulled down her shorts; there was a lot of blood. Both Stacy and her mother were shocked.

"Nikki, you didn't know you started your cycle?"

"No, ma. I had no clue. I thought it was natural," Stacy replied in a whisper.

"Did you wake up bleeding?"

"Yes, mama."

Stacy's mother grabbed her hands and took her to her bedroom. She pulled the bed covers. The bedspread had a large stain of dried blood.

"Chris," Stacy's mother called out to Stacy's father. She continued when he came, "Nikki started the cycle. I need you to go to the store and get some pads, please."

"Are you sure she's still pure?" He asked Stacy's mother, but before she could say anything, he asked Stacy, "Who is the little boy you have brought to your room?"

"No one." Stacy replied. She knew she wouldn't be believed anyway.

Once Stacy's father got back from the store, she cleaned up and sat down for dinner. Her father kept staring at her as if she was dirty. She knew he was onto her and hadn't believed that she had had no boy over.

"I'll make sure. Watch me." He warned Stacy.

Stacy knew he wanted to hurt her, or worse. She only wanted him not to pull out her insides. She was scared he might put his monster inside of her, so she prayed to God, *Oh God, please help me. If I've done something bad, I apologize.*

He pulled out his fingers from her insides and put them in her mouth. "Doesn't it taste good?" He asked.

Stacy didn't answer. She didn't like the taste, though it wasn't bad. *It doesn't taste like Lisa*, she thought.

He pulled out his fingers from her mouth and pushed her face toward his dick.

"Suck it till it explodes," he ordered.

Stacy took all of him in her mouth. She rotated her tongue around his hard dick. She knew how to make this ordeal finish fast. She pulled, sucked, and licked all over it. He moaned loudly. With a few jerks, he came into her mouth.

Stacy wanted to throw up.

"Spit it out and I'm going to beat your ass." He warned. "Now swallow it!"

Stacy found it hard to swallow. It was so thick. He could see Stacy was finding it difficult, so he kept his hand over her mouth.

"Swallow it, dammit!" He whispered aggressively.

Stacy opened up her throat and down it went. She had swallowed it. She couldn't believe it.

"That's more like it! No mess. Now go to sleep," he told her.

"I cannot go clean myself up?"

"You have swallowed it, there's no need to go to the bathroom, right?"

Stacy felt confused.

"Go to sleep. If you get up, I'll know."

Where the hell is this end that my mother kept beating hopelessly in my head, she wondered. It wasn't coming fast enough.

Stacy woke up with strange noises from her mother.

"Stop it, Chris." She yelled. "Stop it! You're going to break my foot. You're evil! Stop it!"

She kept screaming for a while. Then, there was momentary silence and the tables had turned.

The door to Stacy's parent's room busted open with a loud thump.

"Bitch! What the fuck are you trying to do?" Her father came out of the room screaming.

"You bastard! You want to pull my toenails with pliers? You need to die, damn it!" Stacy's mother shrieked.

"Oh shit!" Her father screamed hysterically. "Where did you get that butcher knife from? You crazy bitch! Put it down!"

Chapter 12 - Therapy

"From this moment on, you have so many alternatives, Nikki."

"Nope!" She didn't let Dr. Shawna finish. "I'm not taking any crazy Tic Tacs. I'm sorry. I'll listen to what you have to say, along with keeping up my visits and journaling. But I refuse to pop any wacky enhanced chewable." I can understand taking something for anxiety.

Stacy has attended many therapy sessions to deal with her PTSD. This was just one of those recent appointments with Dr. Shawn. Stacy has been working with her for a while and can now express her thoughts and emotions much better.

Cutting and Hiding happens rarely now, if ever. Stacy has learned to relate to her emotions, but coping with them, at times, can still be a challenge.

"There's so much out there you can take to get you out of that funk you're having," Dr. Shawn started.

Dr. Shawn is a health fanatic with vitamins, exercise, meditation, yoga, and medication, a caring hot mess of joy. Stacy will complain, but she will not miss her virtual appointments. She believes there is no shame in saying one needs help because if Stacy didn't luck up and get an appointment with Dr. Shawn, she doesn't know what she'd do.

So, Stacy follows through on therapy suggestions, but if she doesn't like them, she tells Dr. Shawn, "Next!" When Stacy says that Dr. Shawn knows Stacy won't even try the suggestion.

They have a great doctor-patient vibe, though. Stacy acknowledges how much Dr. Shawn has helped her in her many crises. Following her advice on sticking to a healthy regimen has especially worked wonders for Stacy. However, she has been told that if she wanted to have somewhat of a normal life, she would have to get to the root of everything.

"Are you willing to take something to…"

Stacy interrupted her mid-sentence. "No. No. No is my final answer. I'm used to it. I grew up crazy so it's part of my personality now. Next!"

Dr. Shawn knew she couldn't nudge Stacy once she spoke the word 'next.' She suggested it because she believed it would help motivate Stacy. But Stacy didn't need motivation; she needed sanity.

"You need an energy boost," Dr. Shawn pushed on with her theories. "You should start taking vitamins or a B-12 shot. I've heard that works."

Both started laughing, enjoying the humor.

Going back and forth to a doctor to speak of her issues irritates Stacy. Every time, Dr. Shawn says, "Write down what you're feeling, then we will talk about it during our next session."

Keeping a journal was like dredging up the past. As if she didn't have enough stress already, she'd be in a constant state of worry, hoping no one comes across her hidden past on her laptop. How royally screwed up would she be then? *The hard ass has a secret journal. Oh yeah! Now we know why she's such a bitch and flips out in the head. Really? How wonderful!*

The therapy session ended. Stacy left and, as she sat in her car, experienced an anxiety attack. She recalled her therapist's words: "Your childhood was applauding, which left you with lifelong PTSD to the point you would pass out. The gravity of it all caused you to have epilepsy petit mal seizures. Your childhood experiences often flood your mind, and you can relive sequences of being tortured by your tormentor (your father). You still haven't let it go completely."

Chapter 13 - Closure

Stacy took a summer trip to the West Coast when she was fifteen. She took the trip to visit a foster family to prepare herself to give birth to her child. The father of Stacy's daughter, who was her own abusive, drug-addicted father, didn't even accompany her. All he said was, "Don't talk to strangers and get on the right flights. Bye."

While she was there, Stacy took classes to add credit to finish her junior year of high school and start her senior year so she could finish school on time.

It gave her a year to spend with her daughter before she went back home. She didn't want to go, but she had a scholarship, and she didn't want to lose the chance to get away from her family. Leaving her daughter with her foster parents was one of the most difficult things Stacy has ever done.

Her visit was also cut short by a wedding for which she was a bride's maid. She had to prepare for it, for which she needed to get back to GA.

The fact that life had changed, but she had to continue it as if it hadn't pissed Stacy off. There was no care, no concern for her or her daughter. Stacy knew she could leave and no one would care, that it didn't matter to anyone what happened to her. .

No one said anything. She thought about the moments she had been absent from, when they hadn't seen her for a while, for a year. Maybe they never asked because her parents were so draining; maybe nobody wanted to hear from them or talk to them. Everyone found it a blessing to dissociate themselves. Who cares about children being collateral damage?

So did they never know what was going on? Or did they avoid knowing? Did they ever try to know if the children needed help? Maybe what happens in the family does stay in the family.

Things seemed to change between Stacy and her father around the time of her high school graduation. It was exciting yet dramatic for her. She had finally gotten a peek into her father's feelings toward her.

"Where is she?"

"What?"

"Where is she?"

Heat, liquid heat went through Stacy's body. *No, he didn't just ask where she is,* she told herself. "Why?"

"She's my daughter, and Barb and I are going to raise her."

Stacy burst out laughing loud. "No, you're not, Chris."

"What did you just call me?"

Stacy stood up straighter and repeated, "No, you're not, Chris."

He smacked Stacy at her graduation in front of a small group of people before she had lined up for the ceremony. Stacy never got in line; she turned around and started walking to her car.

As he followed, he said, "Don't walk away from me, Black."

"Where is my daughter?"

Stacy replied loudly, "You mean my sister I had by you, my father, at fifteen?"

He ran up to Stacy and tried to place his hand over her mouth. Stacy started running so he couldn't get a good grip on her.

"What are you trying to do, Black?"

"That's not my name damn it!"

"You think you're grown?"

"How would you know? You haven't provided for me in a while."

He stared at her.

"And don't ever mention my daughter ever again with your mouth. You will never see her or get to know anything about her."

"I have rights…as a father."

"You have nothing!"

"I will take you to court."

Stacy laughed. "You'd be a fool to do it, but if you want, okay. See you, then. I will be waiting to be served. Bye."

Stacy turned and walked away.

He had thought she was going to bow down to him. Hell no!

Stacy worked various jobs, as a teacher, in a children's toy factory, and as a school bus driver; she even wanted to become a professional singer at some point, but in a group who sang for God, though God pushed the group in another direction. No matter what she did, Stacy always had one little person on her mind. Nobody knew she was Stacy's main concern. Everything felt temporary because in six to eight months, she would be gone and nobody would even remember her name.

Once she graduated high school, Stacy went to college for nursing. She had her daughter to think, and she wasn't going to be like how her own mother was toward her; non-existent and oblivious to any and everything.

Being away from her daughter kept a heavy weight on her heart, but Stacy's main concern was always working to provide for her. Whenever she could get to the West Coast to see her, she was there. She couldn't expose anything about her childhood because Stacy wanted to protect her daughter and her foster parents; they had become such a big part of her life to keep her safe. Stacy's father didn't know who was helping her and her daughter.

When Stacy got married, her father was the last person on Earth she wanted to share the good news with. While her father did meet her husband a year after her wedding, she felt no need to talk to him on this occasion, just as she didn't feel the need to talk to him at several other important moments in her life.

She didn't feel guilty about it. She was merely following his example. She became an absentee daughter and did nothing. She felt nothing, too.

She reached out to him seven years after he met her husband. She didn't know why she did it; perhaps she was looking for something from him, closure, or maybe the answer to "Why me?"

Later, while she was traveling, Stacy was diagnosed with cervical cancer. It was then that she asked her father to see her. She wanted to know if he would be concerned.

He told her to count on him if she needed anything. But this gesture didn't move Stacy at all. She didn't need his support; she didn't expect any support from anyone but herself.

Her daughter stayed on the West Coast because Stacy didn't want to disrupt her stable life. As she grew up, she did ask about her father and knew that her mother was raped by a family member, but that worked only for a while. Stacy wonders if the sins that happened upon the mother fall upon the daughter as well.

Was it because she hadn't forgiven him? Stacy realized that even if he didn't acknowledge anything he had done to her, it was vital for her and her father to clear the air for her sake.

So she took it upon herself to call him and ask, "Do you have time to talk to your daughter?"

He answered as loud as he could in a husky voice, "Yes, I have all the time in the world for you, baby girl."

She hated it when he called her by that name. It brought back many disturbing memories.

When she drove up to his house, he met her in his front yard before she had even made it to the door. He had a gigantic smile on his face and he hugged her tightly.

What the heck!

"I can't believe this is happening. My baby girl is in front of me, in my arms," was the first thing he said.

"Stop calling me that, please."

Her words shocked her. A memory of a smack she was given once flashed into her mind. But he was not the well-maintained man she had known growing up. She couldn't believe her heart pounded so hard.

"I really detested you growing up, Dad!" She said it so fast she hoped he didn't hear her.

"Wow!"

Stacy felt extremely uncomfortable with his arms around her. He had heard her clearly, yet walked her into the house with his muscular arms still wrapped around her.

"I wanted you, baby girl...I apologize...Nikki, I wanted you to grow up not depending on anyone to make you happy but yourself," he explained in a heavy voice.

"What a fucking way to indoctrinate me and show me about life," she spat.

"You may have known you deserved a better grade, raise, or respect, but it's up to the individual holding the key to determine that for you, unfortunately, in this world we live in. So, walk away with your head held high and your pride intact," he explained.

What gratification was she supposed to learn?

"So, I raised you to be tough and push and motivate yourself to be aggressive. I alienated you from myself, and it wasn't my intention to hurt you."

"But you did.

It was evident that the life he led had left an awful residue on him and, most of all, Stacy.

He continued the conversation, explaining how he found his marriage to be difficult. He never knew what to do, but he went about it the wrong way. He also touched on some pivotal moments from his military career that haunted him for the rest of his days. He didn't want to go into details of those moments at the time.

"That's our next conversation, baby girl, oops, Nikki," he told Stacy with a defeated smile.

Tears rolled down Stacy's face, which made her father tear up as well. He seemed genuinely apologetic and regretful. He kept holding Stacy's hands and telling her, "I love you, Nikki."

The foul thing was he never acknowledged her, well, their daughter. Yet, if he had brought her up, Stacy would have knocked him to the ground.

Did she see her dad or just the part he wanted her to see—a part she had never seen growing up?

In some sad way, her heart needed to hear those words. "I love you." The words rang through her heart and soul, and they still do to this very day.

It was a difficult day, strange and unexpected, but Stacy had finally learned to release herself from her past.

She felt light, liberated, and free. Stacy realized she was just holding on to anger and resentment toward herself that she had felt from others. Though Stacy was able to walk away from those who never assisted her and was quite generous in her ability to forgive others, it was harder for her to exonerate herself. Thus, she didn't need to forgive her father; she had to forgive herself.

Chapter 14 - A Lesson in Forgiveness

Looking toward a future where her father wasn't a part of her life was a much-needed adjustment for Stacy.

The feeling of instability somewhat dissipated. She had learned that he didn't know how to express his emotions, and he would always struggle with experiences—experiences that caused him mental and physical suffering.

She couldn't say that she had any admiration for her dad, but at least he made himself clear on how he felt about her, now and even back then.

In his own twisted way, he molded, or rather transformed, a defeated child into the strong-willed, motivated, and stubborn woman she is today.

Stacy couldn't stomach it or had the ability to talk about anything more with her father. So, she kept her focus on her upcoming visit to the west coast on Mother's Day.

Stacy knows those reading her story must wonder if she still thinks of her father on Mother's Day. Well, no. Does she think of her mother on that day? No. Does she think of them on their birthdays? Sadly, no.

When Stacy left home, she was only a few months from turning seventeen. She was headed to college. She really left home at fourteen to have a child, so no, she doesn't think of them much. Her parents were long gone from her life.

But the last time she saw both her parents was when she was seventeen, an adult. She saw her father next after ten or eleven years and her mother the same year, only later. This was when Stacy's mother tried to set her on fire. Yes, that's another story. There are many more stories from her life that she is holding on to… that define who she is.

In 2013, Stacy heard of her mother committing suicide. She doesn't know any details of the incident. She is numb to the entire ordeal of her life.

They said their goodbyes, Stacy and her father. And as she walked back toward her car, Stacy felt she had finally found him. She had found the 'dad' in her father after all these years. Yet, at that same moment, it became very clear to her that her life was filled with goodbyes and that they hurt every time.

She felt like she had lost so much. All she knew was that there must be a divine point to it all, and it must be somewhere she couldn't reach, somewhere far away.

Perhaps everything will become clear after she dies. Or maybe it still won't have a point even then. Sometimes, she thought there wasn't any point to it at all.

The only thing that was clear to her was that her childhood was a great disappointment and that no one left this world without feeling immense pain. In the end, if there were no divine explanation, well, that would be truly regretful.

Two weeks later, on Mother's Day 2004, Stacy was all set to visit her daughter on the West Coast. They were supposed to leave later that night.

She was really looking forward to the visit. But the universe always knew when she needed a kick in the ass. Just as she was ready to leave, Stacy received a call from her younger sister that their father was found dead from a heart attack in his home.

Later, she found out that it was from a heroin overdose. He was 55 years old and still chasing the dragon. Some good-bye come when you least expect it.

She never would have thought their beginning would come to an end so soon. Why?

Her father was a man who enforced the law, so he made it a point to oversee how he wanted to live his life.

Stacy didn't know how to feel about his demise. Her emotions were jumbled up, and all forms of feelings felt illegal.

Though this tragedy happened years ago, Stacy still finds herself dazed whenever she thinks of her misunderstood, strong, assertive, and, in the end, very off-putting father.

The tragedy of her life gave her a newfound sight, but the truth changes color depending on the light it's under. Perhaps tomorrow will be clearer than yesterday.

Memories are just a selection of images. Some are elusive, while others are printed on the brain. Every image is like a thread, woven together to tell a story. This thread told the story of Stacy's past.

Stacy's life was like a chessboard, and the player opposite her was time. If she hesitated to move or neglected to move quickly, her piece would be wiped off the board in time. So, the entire time, she has been playing against herself, a partner who will not tolerate indecision. She realized it made no sense to hold on to hatred.

The sad thing is that she had been programmed and manipulated at an early age not to trust anyone. So now, Stacy is learning to release that tension on the lines called life, inch by inch, every day. She will tell you it's not easy, but she can take a deeper breath every day.

Forgiving her father was the most difficult thing Stacy had ever had to do, especially when she was younger. He had a personality that was unwilling to surrender.

You see, love is an expression of one's feelings toward another, but this was something he would not allow himself to show. Like the changing seasons, his attitude would come and pass.

In life, things always happen for a reason, be it wonderful or disastrous. Stacy realized that it takes time to let go of resentment toward anyone.

Forgiveness was a lesson in life. A lesson she had learned when she least expected it. Pondering over it now, Stacy's life taught her to learn leniency. This was the lesson she learned in forgiveness.

Forgiveness was a lesson in Stacy's life,
but not the only lesson.

If you want to know more of Stacy's life
stories, pick up her second book
Beyond Forgivess: The Unforgotten Whispers